D1614138

SUN VALLEY

ARCHITECTURE AND INTERIORS

SUN VALLEY

ARCHITECTURE AND INTERIORS

ALAN EDISON AND JO RABJOHN

FOREWORD BY MARIEL HEMINGWAY

PHOTOGRAPHY BY TIM BROWN

Gibbs Smith, Publisher
Salt Lake City

First Edition

10 09 08 07 06   5 4 3 2 1

Published by

Gibbs Smith, Publisher

P.O. Box 667

Layton, Utah 84041

1.800.748.5439 orders

www.gibbs-smith.com

Designed by Gabriella Hunter

Printed and bound in Hong Kong

Library of Congress Cataloging-in-Publication Data

Edison, Alan.

   Sun Valley architecture and interiors / Alan Edison and Jo Rabjohn.— 1st ed.

        p. cm.

   ISBN 1-58685-517-4

   1. Vacation homes—Idaho—Sun Valley. 2. Interior decoration—Idaho—Sun Valley. 3. Sun Valley (Idaho)—Buildings, structures, etc. I. Rabjohn, Jo. II. Title.

NA7575.E34 2006

720.9796'32—dc22

2005025786

For my children, Rosamond Edison and Cody Edison. I am truly proud to be your father.
Your superior intelligence and wonderful sense of humor make your old man look good.   AE

To my extraordinary daughters, Blair and Ana, who have never ceased to encourage me.   JKR

CONTENTS

F O R E W O R D

BY MARIEL HEMINGWAY

1940s original Union-Pacific–Sun Valley travel poster.

S un Valley, and Ketchum in particular, has always been special to me and I think that I can speak for others when I include those of us who really live here. This is one of the most stunning places on the planet. While most of us have traveled to various parts of the world, we keep coming back to our "home."

The Valley's beauty is not at first overwhelming. There's a hidden beauty that once revealed is undeniable. Our mountains are rugged and primitive. They do not have the grandeur of mountains in other states or countries; they are basic in their majesty. Like a familiar old shirt, there's a comfort in seeing the boulders as you head north on Highway 75 that's always reassuring. However, you have to have spent time in the nurture of this particular environment to be able to truly see it; it's like a spell that slowly unveils its magic after a time of careful observation. The observation is not by your eyes—Mother Earth herself decides when she will reveal herself to you.

In spring and summer, the trails that vein the hills are filled with rambunctious wild flowers and a mixture of pine, pungent sage and putrid cow pile smells. The earth is dry and the streams are cold. While visitors might find this odor distasteful and the landscape uninviting, we true Valley locals find it purely delightful.

The trample of sheep in the early morning of a cool June day causes a welcome delay in getting to our favorite hiking trail. In the more threatening cool of an early September morning, we once again experience this same delay. It is through these types of experiences that we perceive the coming of a season or the gentle reminder of a memory that's been lost.

Every mountain path has a story, and one that completes the reason why we reside here. The stories are different and yet they are based in a devotion to an environment we understand. We love our unique outdoors because it is a constant. So far, the Valley has been able to remain just a hair off being "hip" so that those of us who call it home can live here knowing that whatever wave of "hip-ness" passes through here comes and goes while we remain unchanged.

Above: *The Big Wood River provides outdoor recreation during the warmer months.*
Opposite: *1948 U.S. Women's Olympic Ski Team races.*

We continue to love the Valley like a parent loves an ill-behaved child. The aromas never change and the terrain remains similar, although altered by the demonstrative, and sometimes angry,

"Greetings from Sun Valley, Idaho."

seasons. We honor that nature and hence it pays no attention to us when we pray for better snow or more rain or an Indian summer. Just when we think we can rely on what we are so certain is going to happen, a mid-summer freeze comes along and all our carefully nurtured flowers die.

We are always humbled by the Idaho mountain weather. We learn to expect very little and embrace what we are given. Daunting snowstorms that promise weeks of untracked snow—not to mention the sales of many large homes—followed by a week of rain and an icy month where we learn that carving is necessary regardless of the length and width of our skis.

Early spring can be a tiresome two months of longing for warmth when a gasp of the biggest snowstorm of the season hits. There is a sigh of defeat as our mud tracking, tail-wagging dogs of all breeds leap giddily onto our newly slip-covered couches. It is acceptable, though, because we know of no other place to spend our most memorable occasions, not to mention our least memorable ones as well.

We almost always choose Sun Valley for our special holidays and even when we just need a breather from another home somewhere else. We can't seem to help ourselves. We love it here and the Valley loves us back. We always pay reverence to the Valley's show. In this theater of cold, hot, dry or flooded, lies the land that we adore. We're certain not to miss an encore. However, if we do, we promise ourselves that we will return when the work outside is done because we must return to the arms of our less than graceful home since it has become our own nature.

The nearby Guyer Hot Springs attracted tourism and many lodges were constructed to accommodate them.

The Valley will either become the place you call your own or you may be one of those who comes and is never able to see what we locals can't stop seeing—the rugged peaks on all sides of our valley that envelop our hearts. We are protected by the Sawtooths, the Pioneers, the White Clouds and, of course, by our "all activity" friend, Mount Baldy. There is no choice but to embrace the hills and the rivers and all of the gifts, good and bad, that they bless us with.

If you decide not to stay, that's OK. We'll be here if you return. ✸

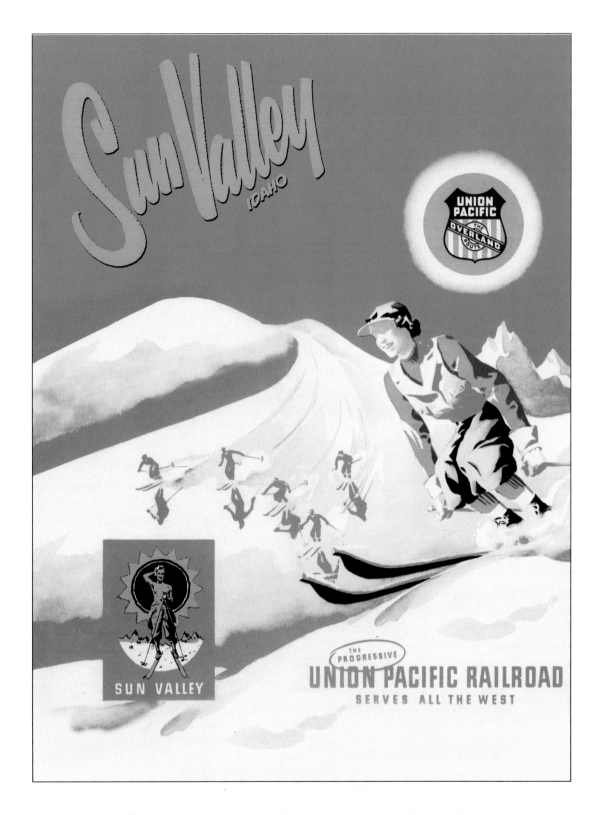

Original Union-Pacific–Sun Valley travel poster. Early posters promoted the fabulous skiing in the area.

Original Union-Pacific–Sun Valley travel poster, "Round House."

INTRODUCTION

A natomy may be destiny but location can have divine decree, and the Wood River Valley was predetermined to enchant. Count Felix Schaffgotsch, when scouting for the perfect setting for his European-style destination ski resort, said it had "More delightful features of any place I've seen." At its conception, elegance became a permanent facet of the area, and Sun Valley continues attracting clientele of East Coast notables and Hollywood stars. All bring a wealth of style and creativity to the community, and express themselves in their homes and lifestyles. Sun Valley is a geographic ideal, a gem in a perfect setting. Since it became popular in the 1930s, the unique blend of wild places and civilization ensured that Sun Valley would continue to flourish. Its neighbor Ketchum has been equally prosperous.

Original postcard. Duck pond and Challenger Inn.

Because many of the wealthy clientele enjoyed Sun Valley and Ketchum so much, it seemed logical for them to build vacation homes there because of the frequency of their visits. The style of Sun Valley became one based upon recreation—it is a pendulum swinging between opulence and simplicity. The vacation spirit is here regardless of season, and pursuits such as fishing, hiking, skiing, biking or relaxation take precedence. The natural surroundings give life a gaiety, and weather, no matter what type, is taken with excitement and anticipation of what it will bring. Residents and visitors find delight in skiing newly powdered slopes, enjoying crisp fall evenings, riding a bicycle over fallen leaves, or casting for trout on an early summer morning. This vacation joy is expressed in a relaxed comfortable style unique to Sun Valley. As famous New York designer Billy Baldwin said, "Some people confuse luxury with grandeur. To me comfort is perhaps the ultimate luxury."

This book is devoted to the variety of architecture and design, art and artistry that make up Sun Valley style. From modern homes constructed of iron and glass to long-lasting rustic fishing cottages, each place celebrates the style because it is infused with the personalities of its owners. For some, grandeur and luxury are their signature style, while for others, whimsy and eclecticism abound. Common loves and choices seem to have melded all.

Alan Edison and Jo Rabjohn

HISTORY OF SUN VALLEY

KC 72 Boulder Mts., Idaho

Opposite: Original black and white promotional photo. "Powder Day on Baldy."
Above: Vintage panoramic postcard. "The Boulder Mountains."

S un Valley is an oasis between desert and lava of the Snake River Plain, an isolated haven and difficult place to reach from just about anywhere. It is wedged between surrounding peaks of Sawtooth, Smokey and Boulder Ranges with a high desert climate. In recent years, the Wood River Valley has grown into a year-round resort destination, with tourism dominating the local economy as people from around the globe come to enjoy the abundance of nature found there.

However, a different kind of natural abundance drew the first influx of people from elsewhere. The Hudson's Bay Company sent Alexander Ross as head of a large expedition to trap beaver in the area in 1824. Ross's journal is the first-known written record of this region. After a less than pleasant hike over Trail Creek Summit on June 17, 1828, the expedition passed through what is now Sun Valley.

"We found the climate changed for the better, the snow off the ground, the weather warm, and the grass fully long. Late in the evening we reached a stream running through a deep valley in the direction of the southwest. . . . on its east bank we encamped at a late hour."

That was the Big Wood River and the late-night campsite is now West Ketchum. "In the vicinity of our present encampment were the finest appearances of beaver we had yet seen," and Ross goes on to say, ". . . the place was promising, the weather fine and the grass good, so that our worn out horses both fed and rested." The Ross party stayed in its encampment in Ketchum for four days and nights, surviving an encounter with a large party of Blackfoot from Elkhorn before leaving to move downriver and across Camas Prairie. For a few more decades, the area was left mostly to the native people.

Nearly fifty-five years later, in 1879, treasure-seeking prospectors discovered gold, lead and silver ores. David Ketchum operated a pack team to serve prospectors and arriving merchants. He built a small shelter along Trail Creek, the first structure in what is now Ketchum.

Vintage 1930s postcard. "Cowboy on Horse in the Big Wood River."

Following in 1880, Isaac Lewis arrived in the area, bringing "all the necessary tools and equipment for a genuine prospect and mining outfit"; he settled in and stayed long enough to build several of the brick buildings that are still standing in Ketchum. His diary gives a picture of Ketchum's beginnings as a town.

"On the morning of May 3, 1880, at about 11:00, we pitched our tent on the present site of the town of Ketchum. The party that came the day before did not raise a tent. They marked off on a piece of brown paper a kind of plat with blocks and lots numbered, and had struck stakes in the snow to represent where the main street was. They held a meeting among themselves and called the place Leadville. They appointed a man by the name of Sterling as secretary and town recorder, with the power to record one lot for each resident for the sum of two dollars. We took up four lots and I paid Mr. Sterling eight dollars before we had our tent up. This was the first expenditure of money by any person on the present site of Ketchum."

These same lots sell for approximately one million dollars today.

The U.S. Post Office turned down the name Leadville because of its overuse as a town name in the West. The populace decided to honor David Ketchum and name the town after him, for he was one of the "outstanding characters of the county on account of his personality . . . and he had a kindly, genial disposition but not one to take liberties with." After two weeks, several hundred people had reached the site and Ketchum was officially a tent city. It didn't take long before permanent structures were built, and some still remain. Vast quantities of rich ore enticed businesses to start mining in the area.

Life in Ketchum was never dull during its boom days. The *Ketchum Keystone* reported nonchalantly in 1885, "a great week for killings and births, the former in a preponderance!" The *Idaho Tri-Weekly Statesman* of Boise reported, "All day long, and far into the night, men from every quarter of the globe, bronzed and bearded miners, merchants, professional

Left: *Original photograph (ca 1920). Main Street of Ketchum looking north.*
Right: *1920s photograph. Ketchum Kamp Saloon & Hotel, Main Street.*
Opposite: *Sun Valley Depot (ca 1930–1940). End of the line.*

Original black and white photograph. After hours, ski instructors provide the entertainment, Bavarian style, in the Ram Bar.

Original postcard. "Dog Sled in Back of Sun Valley Lodge, 1937."

Original photograph. State-of-the-art buses drop off skiers at the end of the day.

men, uncouth bull-whackers, profane mule skinners, quartz experts, stock sharps, gamblers and desperados crowd the sidewalks and throng the saloons." A series of mine strikes brought $60 million in lead, silver and gold and made the region Idaho's leading mining area. In 1883, the railroad arrived and by the end of 1884, Ketchum supported thirteen saloons, four restaurants, six livery stables, two banks, a bookstore, drugstore, brewery, lumber yard, fruit stands and a weekly paper. However, when the silver market collapsed in 1894, the mining industry declined in Sun Valley and throughout the West. Residents left to find other sources of income, and only 10 percent of the population remained.

Original postcard. "Grandeur of Baldy Mountain."

The railway service to Ketchum was what kept Ketchum alive after the loss of the boom-time population. Elizabeth L. Singer, a resident during that period, described life in Sun Valley in the years just before World War I:

> "The tempo of life in Ketchum was dull. . . . Wages were low and winter jobs were scarce. Work at the Independence Mine up East Fork was the main source of mining employment. Summer jobs usually consisted of part time work with the forest service on fire fighting control or work at the saw mills . . . the work was from early spring until late fall—all depending on snow conditions. A few jobs were available with the county for road maintenance after the building of graded roads began. There was no unemployment compensation . . . it was a matter of making your summer earnings last through the winter and hope for a good job after spring opened up."

Ms. Singer recalled the people who populated Ketchum in its early days:

> "In spite of all this [hardship], the people were contented. Most families had an equity on a small home. Heat was supplied with wood gathered each summer or early fall . . . there were no street lights to brighten your way around town, only the lights of the family dwellings along the street . . . life went on serenely though. People were self-sufficient at meeting their problems and creating their own diversions."

Opposite: *Original photograph (ca 1950). A dog sled gives happy lodge visitors a ride around the snow-filled grounds.*

Above: *Original poster. A lift ride offers a quiet moment before the drama of downhill skiing.*

Ketchum residents in need of a doctor had to travel to Hailey eleven miles south, and the round-trip journey took all day. Three times a week, the train was available and was the only means of transportation out of the snowbound village. Dog sleds were often used as an alternative. Although the economic hardships were rough for those at the time, it was a blessing in disguise because the land was left relatively untouched from the ravages of the mining industry.

Looking up Main Street on a summer day in the 1960s.

Shepherds replaced miners, and the Sun Valley/Ketchum area became one of the world's top sheepherding centers, second only to Sydney, Australia. Most of the herders were Basque emigrants and the sheep industry brought a substantial Basque influence to the valley, while today the international influence in this industry comes from immigrating Peruvians. Still today in Sun Valley, the seasons can be marked by the moving of the herds from pasture to mountain meadows through neighborhoods and along Highway 75. The bucolic scene of shepherds on foot and horseback accompanied by their working dogs nipping heel and hoof is a delightful sight to all who live here.

As automobiles became popular in the 1920s, the newfangled transportation easily carried tourists into the valley. Yet the Ketchum population was just 270 in 1935 and fewer than 100 during the winter. In 1936, Averell Harriman served as the chairman of the Union Pacific Railroad. Seeking to increase passenger service, he decided an alpine ski center would be an ideal stimulus to tourism. He sent Austrian ski champion Count Felix Schaffgotsch to find the perfect setting of dry powder snow on open treeless slopes sheltered by higher mountains and not too strenuous an elevation. The count visited many areas, including Alta, Utah; Jackson Hole, Wyoming; Yosemite Valley, California; Mt. Rainier, Washington; and Mt. Hood, Oregon; but none fit the criteria envisioned by Harriman. Count Schaffgotsch of Austria was boarding a train in Colorado to return to New York to report a failure to find a site when an Idaho official of the Union Pacific Railroad contacted him. He urged the count to try one last area—Ketchum, Idaho. Fortunately the count took his advice and boarded another train bound for Idaho. Although he had been courted by community officials throughout the West and treated to the best accommodations and meals, the reception in Ketchum was different. When merchant Jack Lane was informed of the party's arrival, he promptly sent word out to his associates, "Don't cash any of his checks!"

Having turned down Aspen as being too high in elevation, Schaffgotsch found Dollar Mountain fit the bill because of the relatively gentle foothills of the Sawtooths. He said, "Among the many attractive spots I have visited, this combines more delightful features of any place I have seen in the United States, Switzerland or Austria for winter sports resorts." Within three days after arriving at Sun Valley, Schaffgotsch was authorized to purchase Brass Ranch, one mile east of Ketchum.

Above: *Original promotion photograph. "Skier walks towards the Opera House."*

Opposite: *Original hand-colored photograph. "A Western Welcome to Sun Valley."*

A beautiful Sun Valley poster shows 1940s skiers in the most fashionable ski attire.

Looking to attract summer tourists in the early 1940s, Union-Pacific created this color poster featuring the ice ring's pro, Audrey Peppe.

A contemporary poster depicts an all-American sportswoman flyfishing in the Big Wood River.

On a glorious summer day, a tourist rides up the Baldy Mountain chairlift.

Engineers and construction crews flocked to the area and construction began in May of 1936. The name *Sun Valley* was chosen because the snow remained on the ground, even in the brightest winter sun, and early brochures showed tanned skiers, some naked to the waist.

The developers wanted to create an idealized community nestled in the wilderness. Miners and ranchers may have been here first, but Harriman envisioned something that hadn't been here previously. He modeled his Idaho resort after the look and feel of Austrian alpine villages. He recruited ski instructors and chefs from Europe to help flesh out the idyllic Tyrolean landscape. In the early planning, the idea of "roughing it in luxury" was promoted and has remained a constant theme ever since. "It is not enough to build a hotel and then mark with flags and signs the things you propose to do in time to come," Harriman said. "When you get to Sun Valley, your eyes should pop open. There isn't a single thing I could wish for that hasn't been provided." Even then, the contradiction of rustic and luxurious, active and relaxed, strenuous and sumptuousness came together to create a unique style.

On December 21, 1936, just eleven months and five days after Count Schaffgotsch had first arrived in Ketchum, Sun Valley Resort opened to international publicity. Upon completion of the Sun Valley Lodge and the Sun Valley Inn, the resort boasted ". . . timber-free slopes covered with powder snow. Brilliant sunshine, windless days made possible skiing stripped to waist." In addition, ". . . outdoor bathing in a warm-water pool—ice tanning in sun-room igloos." Also on-site was a ski shop that was run and stocked by Saks Fifth Avenue.

The resort opening attracted an elite and exclusive crowd. Those listed in social registers on both coasts as well as the stars of the Hollywood screen were all sought after as clientele. "The persons who're going to Sun Valley . . . are those who set the styles and [determine] what is and isn't fashionable in clothes, liquor, travel, recreation and resorts," reported the December 20, 1936, *Idaho Daily Statesman* of Boise. That image established from the beginning endures today.

Original artwork (ca 1930). Horse and rider looking over the town of Ketchum.

In 1977, Sun Valley came under the ownership of R. Earl Holding, and since then he has redefined the standard of elegance and excellence subscribed by Harriman. Sun Valley Lodge and Sun Valley Inn have been lavishly refurbished. Profound improvements from the stairs and halls to guest rooms have increased the Mount Baldy amenities. But Holding's main accomplishment was what he called the Triple Crown: "Baldy is a regal mountain and it is only fitting that she wear a crown radiant with three precious jewels." The jewels he referred to are Baldy's three award-winning day lodge facilities: Warms Springs Lodge, Seattle Ridge Lodge and River Run Lodge. The most recent addition to the crown is Carol's Dollar Mountain Lodge (named in honor of Earl's wife Carol Holding), a facility devoted to children's ski and snowboard activities.

Above: Original black and white photograph (ca 1960). Six members of the Ski School stand in front of the Sun Valley Lodge.

Opposite: Sun Valley regular Gary Cooper chats to fellow actor Claudette Colbert.

The ranch town of Ketchum absorbed the influence of the resort. Railroad patrons who could afford a vacation and time away from work expected comforts and amenities. Advertising was aimed at the affluent eager for Western excitements and a view of the wilderness. The Austrian-style resort adorned with continental accents, food and costumes was ultimately distilled through American sensibility. *Outside* columnist Randy White wrote that it appeared "a cadre of Swiss watchmakers and team of rodeo hands" designed and constructed Ketchum, neither yielding to the other.

Ketchum, its economic future restored by tourism, retains its pioneer charm, and many of the original buildings still standing provide a view of the romantic past. The residents of Ketchum complain of change and congestion encroaching upon their peaceful and rustic community, but the area remains pastoral. Houses are not allowed on the hills or mountains, which are full of dear, antelope, elk, foxes, badgers and bear. In the Silver Creek Preserve south of Sun Valley, trout grow to eight pounds or more and loiter under bridges, while a moose or two occasionally wander through. Ornithologists from around the world travel to this area for bird-watching. Longtime resident Ernest Hemingway once said of this countryside, "You'd have to come from a test tube and think like a machine to not engrave all of this in your head so that you never lose it."

Today, Sun Valley is often called the best single ski mountain area in the United States. The resort offers 19 lifts, 78 runs, over 3,000 skiable acres and 3,400 vertical feet. When Averell Harriman authorized the expenditure of 1.5 million dollars to build the Sun Valley Lodge in 1936, no one could anticipate the original purchase price would become a fraction of what many of the homes in the valley cost today.

Original travel brochure.

Atop Penny Mountain, adventurers stop to admire the view.

A33~ The Lodge and Ice Rink, Sun Valley

Original postcard (ca 1939). "The year-round ice skating rink."

Union Pacific promotional photograph. World famous skier and instructor, Sigi Engl.

Presently, Sun Valley is considered an equally superior warm weather playground. Bicyclists, in-line skaters, strollers and joggers enjoy paths paralleling the Wood River. Modern anglers wade the same streams that drew Ernest Hemingway and Gary Cooper. Sun Valley offers a wealth of first-class fishing and hunting opportunities. Golfers abound on four courses that combine scenery and technical challenges. The high-speed quad chairlifts that whisk skiers and snowboarders to the top of Bald Mountain in the winter also run in the summer, offering access to cyclists, hikers and sightseers. From town, paragliders can be seen floating off Baldy. The area has truly evolved as a resort for all seasons.

The heated circular outdoor pool in 1950.

Opposite: *Hitting the slopes in 1937, Rocky and Gary Cooper join Clark Gable at the Dollar Mountain ski run.*

Above: *Tourists fish on the shore of Redfish Lake.*

Sun Valley ranks as number eighteen in the *The 100 Best Small Art Towns in America*, and is described there as "a great small art town with a nice balance between the visual arts, theater, and music." For more than thirteen years, the annual Sun Valley Summer Symphony has held their concerts under the tent on the manicured lawn of the Sun Valley Esplanade. The SVSS is the largest privately funded free admission symphony in America. One of the most popular jazz events in the country is the Sun Valley Jazz Festival, which occurs one week after a local festival called the Trailing of the Sheep. This unique celebration involves a parade of Scottish, Basque, Polish and Peruvian displays and dances, ending with the massive herding of sheep through the main street. Art galleries and craft shows showcase national talent, and theater groups perform year-round.

Sun Valley welcomes back visitors year after year with its style of "roughing it in luxury," which has become a tradition for families across the world. As the locals say, "Winter brings you here but summer keeps you coming back." ✺

Starlet Rhonda Fleming gets some tips on the tennis court.

ARCHITECTURE FOR LIFESTYLES

Since the middle of the nineteenth century, the wilderness of the Wood River Valley has been a Native American trapping region, a mining center, and a sheepherding area. But the identity that the world knows is that of one of the world's finest multi-seasonal destination resorts.

Sun Valley is the "grand dame" of skiing in America. Other resorts may have better terrain, deeper snow or bigger verticals, but few can compete with Bald Mountain's diversity of 360-degree exposure, brilliant bowls or dark glades. Other resorts cannot compare with the vast untouched wilderness—unlogged and roadless—or the strong sense of community and collective desire to protect the natural resources. Sun Valley's reputation as a glamorous playground for affluent skiers is rooted in history and the area still attracts celebrities, technology moguls and heirs. In recent decades, the resort has sought to accommodate families from all walks of life who enjoy the outdoors.

Although Sun Valley started as a winter resort, it is now considered an equally superior warm weather playground. Over the past fifteen years, the area has experienced a 50 percent population increase, with year-round residents numbering more than 20,000. The most visible residents are the well-heeled recreationalists. Not so visible are those service industry people, cooks, mechanics, housekeepers and landscapers whose numbers have grown almost 400 percent. As recently as 2003, the average cost of a single family home was $633,389; compared to a state average of $106,000. Today, the average price of a single family home in the area is more than $3 million.

Set within this narrow alpine valley, Ketchum still has the ambiance of an authentic western community. Its style encompasses both the wild and the sophisticated. Faded jeans and dime store work shirts have long since given way to the casually sophisticated look of khaki slacks, polo shirts, Italian loafers and high tech sports attire. Hummers and new SUVs park next to restored pickup trucks.

Sun Valley's spectacular views and easy access to great golf courses, ski runs and the world's best fishing make it easy for people to do what they can to live there. With such a diverse background, it is only natural that the home style and architecture of Sun Valley is as varied as its inhabitants. Yet somehow it all works together to create that unique Sun Valley style. A cutting-edge modern residence can sit comfortably next to a classic log construction. The architecture of the houses reflects the desires to incorporate spectacular views and settings. Homes must be able to withstand a harsh and variable climate that also dictates design and choices of materials. Most of the populace indulges in some sort of outdoor recreation, with their sporting lives apparent in the choice of décor. The resort atmosphere often reduces formal living to a much more relaxed mode, but never undercuts the sophisticated sensibilities. Grand homes have a carefree relaxed environment. Wherever you look, Averell Harriman's vision of roughing it in luxury is maintained and embraced in Sun Valley. ✺

Sun Valley residents have a unique relationship with the outdoors and, large or small, their homes reflect that symbiotic bond.

NATURE OF
RESTRAINT

I n Taoism, it is said, "learning is forgetting," and architect Michael Doty is always careful to learn about the needs and
wants of his clients. So adept in his skills, Doty assimilates the elements of design to such a degree that
the house reflects his client and the site more than his own personality. At this site, he succeeded with a building that
exudes a joie de vivre. For Michael Doty, architecture is for life, pleasure, work and people.

Without looking back at architectural precedent or reverting to a
historic style, Doty began his design by taking advantage of the magnificent views of the river, meadows and mountains. The building
deferred to the natural beauty of the site. One of the keys to inte-
grating the houses with its surroundings is the entrance. The view
cannot be seen upon entering the property and motor court. Not
until you've entered the home through its massive door and gazed
through its 22-foot floor-to-ceiling windows does the wondrous view
become apparent.

Above: Windows dominate the back side of the house incorporating
views and natural lighting.

Opposite: Sitting like a fortress against the elements, this home easily
combats the extremes of the region, from hot summers to frigid winters.

Nature is invited inside through elegant detailing. The 22-foot ceilings make the most of the views, captured through large expanses of glass that agree with the scale of the living and dining rooms. As is standard with contemporary living rooms, particularly those in Sun Valley, the views of mountains and rivers beyond glass walls are as important a living space as the room itself. Nature and structure become integrated as both the interior and exterior are treated as complete entities and then subdivided by rooms for specific purposes. Each room feels a part of the next, and they all combine to create the whole.

The strength of the external shell allows the softness of the interior, painted in soft neutrals, to maximize the sense of space and avoid competition with the view. Organized around an unconventional floor plan, a stone veneer wall runs the entire length of the building and extends beyond, creating a spine. This great wall organizes the traffic flow and divides the house into open and enclosed spaces. The living areas and bedrooms are arranged along the west side to take advantage of the sunlight and views.

The selection of materials and finishes were made with extreme care, with the emphasis given to the art objects. Doty chose to contrast the rough and smooth textures, with the natural offsetting of machine-made materials. The sparseness of the interiors is an economy in choice, made because the space is luxurious by nature. Furniture within this space is simply for function — nothing else is necessary to enhance or complement.

Often in contemporary styling, the elements of structure and furnishings appear similar, and it's difficult to analyze what separates one interior from another as outstanding. Perhaps the key to success is a not to be obviously clever or contrived. The result is a multitude of rooms composed in a casual, comfortable manner, achieving a goal with good design. ☀

Contemporary style is timeless and calming, allowing the exterior views to take center stage.

Above: The massive glass and wood sculpture door creates its own entrance.

Below: A contrast of natural and machine-made materials creates a sculptural staircase.

Opposite: Birch veneer plywood is used for the cabinets and for the suspended ceiling. The flooring is bamboo, and color accent is achieved with stainless steel.

Opposite: The owners incorporated passive solar techniques for taming the harsh high-elevation climate.

Above: Despite the large expanses of glass and the scale of the rooms, there is a real sense of enclosure achieved at night when there are no daylight views.

Below: Windows are placed between the roof edge and the main wall that runs the length of the home.

Above: *A series of plinths creating lawns extend into the landscape and are framed and bordered with the same colored concrete as interior floors.*

Below: *The entrance door, with floors of polished black concrete and bamboo trim, adds instant drama and pause.*

Opposite: *Above the glass-topped great wall, a shed roof with supporting kickers is incorporated to add more light.*

ART AND
ARCHITECTURE

When New York architect Caitlin Moore collaborated with Sun Valley architect Janet Jarvis, their main concern was the distillation of basic shapes to their purest forms. For that reason, this house was raised five feet above the lot to take advantage of both river views and availability of natural light. The decision celebrates order and integrity in the reduction of everything to its purest form. All unnecessary elements have been eliminated or hidden out of sight. Lighting on the exterior and in the front entry was recessed within stonework so fixtures would not hang out.

The purity continues into the interior, with a sparseness of color that provides a gallery-like backdrop for the owner's extensive art collection as well as the outdoor scenery framed with windows. The natural light that is allowed to enter through the dramatic windows creates different moods and expressions depending on the time of day. This mixture of the elements and their no-frills appeal produces an exciting and stylish home. The feelings of endless space and time are achieved with multiple levels and a multipurpose environment. The success and beauty of Moore's work is derived from its ability to convey a lot with a limited vocabulary—the fusion of art and architecture. ✳

Opposite: *Fenestration-framed vignettes of surrounding groves and river at twilight wash the living room in streaks of gold and pink.*

Above: *Organic and industrial materials are united by common shapes.*

Above: *Displaying art in unexpected places adds excitement on surfaces that contribute to textual interest.*

Opposite: *Besides being the focal point of the living room, the great stone fireplace showcases how outside building elements can be used indoors, creating harmony between them.*

Above: *Using materials over and over again, such as the metal in furniture legs and ceiling fans, perfects the composition of the room.*

Opposite: *Repeating visuals of linear patterns are seen in floor planking, railings, rock patterns and window framing. The combination of industrial and natural materials is done by virtue of discernment in simplicity and restraint.*

Opposite: The stone fireplace becomes a focal point enhanced by the showcasing of the owner's extensive art collection.

Above: Clean lines and natural materials combine to create a fresh, uncluttered experience.

Below: Selectivity is evident in the sparseness of the room; cabinets are devoid of knobs, and even the bare wood of the cabinetry lends a feeling of clean simplicity.

Above: *Recessed lighting is hidden within the rock, eliminating the need for outdoor fixtures.*

Below: *The design of the structure repeats the shape of the materials used creating a natural harmony.*

Opposite: *The use of flat rock on the chimney, repeated along the foundation through to wallside and the entry patio, adds texture to a minimal design.*

LESS IS A LOT
MORE WORK

Above: Mystery and glamour envelop the home with the use of night lighting.
Opposite: Above the garage rests the guest quarters, bridged from the main house. The garage door is a steel airplane-hanger door that hinges into an overhang when opened. Natural elements can be seen in wood and stone, blending harmoniously for color and surface texture.

Independent of trend or fashion, this is a one-of-a-kind house shaped by the particular needs and desires of its owners. Three things were stipulated to architect Susan Desko from the beginning of the building project: no logs, no river rock and no maintenance.

Desko designed a home of common and modest materials, uncluttered living spaces and respect for the quiet. She chose materials that were strong and unembellished, such as exposed trusses and joists, which were used specifically because they reveal their naked beauty. The unique home possesses energy and power. When entering through the front door, the sequence of sights and surprises delights the senses—warm light, unexpected textures and uncustomary heights. Every room is magnetic, piquing curiosity and seductively drawing visitors into comfortable seating arrangements.

Desko created the residence with full knowledge of how to effectively integrate various elements to create a fabulous whole, such as the power of natural light, surprising outdoor spaces, proportions within rooms and a boldness of mass and texture.

The home seems to reach for the wide Idaho sky, with 30-foot ceilings in the kitchen and 14-foot doors and windows. Varnished plywood covers the walls in rich wood grain and sliding barn doors are used for closets. Full walls of windows accommodate the scale of trees and mountains. Every window has been fabricated for the design of each room. Views are incorporated and invested with meaning. The relationship of the indoors and outdoors is part of the coherence of design. Not only admitting light, the windows blur distinctions and create vibrant interplay between the inside and the outside. Shadows complement sunlit areas surrounded with shade and an air of mystery. At evening, high windows capture a moonscape intrigue, which plays as large a role as the furnishings.

The major materials expressed and experienced repeat in rhythm, repetition and variation. Devoid of flurry and fluff, the natural beauty, fiber and finish of materials is sufficient and without need for adornment, change of color or texture. Steel is left untreated to change with exposure to the climate and elements. Stacked firewood logs supported by unseen rebar are used as a natural wall around the home. The home is a structure of strength without much need for adornment other than showcasing the owner's art collection. A single overscaled painting will take command of a wall. Dramatic standing lighting fixtures in the living room are sculptures.

A powerful chemistry is created within this home, and the style is both utilitarian and elegant, where everything is an integral part of the design, furnishings and lighting to texture and color of walls and floors. ☀

The concrete island extends from the kitchen into the entry, and storage and appliances were fabricated into the design of the single unit. Walls of windows slide open to experience each season completely, eliminating boundaries with ease.

Above: *The open fireplace leads into the kitchen, a center point for the joining informal den.*

Below: *The dining room and formal living room share space made intimate by specific purpose. Dramatic and well chosen, the room's accessories express character.*

Opposite: *Large in scale but delicate in nature, a painting by Claudia Parducci dominates this room.*

Above: *A stair landing doubles as an office, and the plywood wall on the right slides open to reveal storage, supplies and technical equipment.*

Opposite: *Custom-designed poster beds provide sufficient furnishings for the children's bunk room. Linens were designed to match the construction of the furniture.*

Opposite: *An irrigation pipe is used for the shower head.*

Above: *Glass window walls slide to open the rooms to the outdoors.*

Below: *Mosaic walls mimic the glistening water as it comes pouring from a shower. The poured concrete bath was measured to the precise dimensions of its owner, and this commonsense approach to comfort is accented by industrial pipes and fittings.*

R I V E R
RETREAT

S un Valley isn't exactly halfway between San Francisco and St. Louis, but it is close enough to be selected as the final destination for two sisters and their families. Eleven people share this sprawling retreat tucked within groves of aspen and white birch along the edge of the Big Wood River. It is composed of a main house connected by a covered breezeway to a second dwelling. Architect Serena Stewart had to meet her clients' unique needs of providing two master bedrooms with equal views and appointments. Ultimately, a coin toss made the final determination of bedroom ownership.

What started as a smaller shingled house evolved into a stately log home. The remodel and additions were built to accommodate joint vacations and holidays. Every room has spacious windows to view the river. A solarium was added as a dining room, and an extra benefit of plentiful natural light adds a sense of well-being.

Floor-to-ceiling windows frame a stone fireplace, constructed as a focal point. Irregular ceiling beams run throughout, matched by post stair rails, balustrades and spindles. Hickory, twig and log furniture complement and repeat the pattern of timber construction and rustic décor.

Opposite: Manicured lawns fit right in with the natural landscape of the Big Wood River.

Above: An original 1915 silent movie banner, along with Western memorabilia, is part of the family's large collection of Western art.

The interior resonates with a Western theme, and the whole is a gentle evolution of individual and joint purchases—folk art, Navajo rugs, Thomas Molesworth furniture, vintage movie banners on canvas, and accumulations of just the right hats and horns. Elements of Adirondack and California Rancho décor mix with Native American geometric patterns repeated throughout the residence.

Under a covered heavy log breezeway at a convenient distance, the second structure houses the children's quarters. With bedrooms above, the ground floor houses an inviting den filled with vintage Western movie posters from the 1940s and 1950s, along with cowboy memorabilia.

After years of shared times and experiences, this residence has fulfilled its purpose of providing a place where memories will linger like snapshots, reminding the owners of happy times. ☀

Above: *Whimsical Western objects add to the festive nature of the home.*

Opposite: *Looking out upon the ever-changing river, diners are treated to the best views in the house.*

Opposite: A chipped Adirondack root chair, a 1920s Navajo rug and vintage Wild West show poster add eclectic charisma to the living room.

Above: Avid collectors take a light-hearted approach to deciding what constitutes treasure. The entry hall tree is the depository for a cowboy and fly-fishing hat collection.

Opposite: *The home's log exterior and inviting wraparound porch set the standard for Western hospitality.*

Above: *Geometric prints repeated throughout the house are both practical and compatible with log furnishings and Western décor.*

Below: *Details in a wet bar make fixing a drink nearly as fun as consuming one.*

Above: *Decks connect the children's wing to the main house, allowing privacy in both areas.*

Below: *Incorporation of log construction into outdoor furniture and the use of natural stone for the patio material add to the home's rustic design.*

Opposite: *Log construction is easily adaptable to various additions through the years to accommodate growing families.*

T R U E
WEST

Fashioned after a true western sporting lodge, this home honors both heritage and legacy. The crude hand-hewn beams of raw timber set the stage for the refinements of civilization and the finest of frontier style. Traditional cowboy arts, paintings and sculptures preserve the spirit of ranch life in the Old West, where a good horse and a dependable friend meant survival. From the tradition of true grit to western elegance, a visual theme runs throughout this home—one of pride, heritage, honor, patriotism and gratitude to country.

To remind the owners of their original roots in Santa Barbara, California, Western art adorns the walls, and Visalia saddles of classic vaquero tradition, Santa Barbara bits, and Ortega rawhide are also exhibited. Display cases are filled with fancy bits and spurs that are full-flowered, stamped and sparkling, dazzling buckles of silver and gold, and complex braided cowhide.

Above: A classic silver-mounted Olsen-Nolte saddle along with a martingale and headstall are displayed with paintings of western cowboy life by California artist Edward Borein.

Opposite: All rooms open to the patio overlooking the meadows and Big Wood River.

Rooms are adorned with the spoils of hunt, scenes of the great outdoors and the mystique of adventure. A blend of wildlife, safari and frontier memorabilia decorate the home—firearms cased and cleaned, skins draped across walls, furniture upholstered in hides, and trophies and photos that speak of victories achieved. The romance and ideal of the primitive entwines with privileged sophistication.

Lawns surround the residence all the way to the river's edge. A footbridge allows access to additional guest quarters housed in rustic sheep wagons. The owners and their guests can enjoy outdoor barbecues on the grass, and then retire for the evening by the fireplace in the screened porch, snug on oversized couches framed in hickory log with light from bark-shaded lamps. Heroic symbols of America, vintage flags, patriotic memorabilia, and wartime collectibles decorate this grand place. ☀

Opposite: *Wild trappings, books galore, photos of conquests and relaxing furniture fill the den. Heavy beams and rough-hewn timber add to the masculine atmosphere.*

Above: *European and American West pieces are compatible, using similar animal and adventure themes.*

Above: Across the hall from the master bedroom is an expansive master bath and dressing room adorned with Navajo rugs and early California paintings.

Below: The hallways for this home were designed wider in order to accommodate furniture settings and western displays.

Opposite: The screened-in porch is a welcome hideaway, juxtaposed to the home's oversized rooms and filled with American mementos in a patriotic theme.

This magnificent entry table was created by local Sun Valley artist Doug Tedrow of Wood River Rustics.

The various objects of wood from log walls to the carved table combine in a marriage that exudes Western warmth.

Opposite: *For the more adventurous guest, a converted sheep wagon provides a true Western experience.*

Above: *The extensive collection of Native American Plains Indian beadwork with a flag motif and artifacts celebrates the past.*

Below: *A custom totem pole (36 feet tall) from the Northwest sits at the entrance of the property.*

TIMELESS
HOMESTEAD

E arly mining tales are filled with fancy and romance. Legend tells of a prospector's dog that tore after a rabbit. Both tussled in a thicket, and when the dust settled, the prospector discovered that the animals had unearthed pay dirt of silver ore. When miners descended on the area, the town of Broadford was founded, and the mining township's population grew to 600 by 1884. Millions of dollars in lead and silver were extracted. Sadly, between the changing fortunes of quarrying and the misfortune of fire, only one building remains on the wide ford across the river.

Within 119 acres bordering one of the longest private sections of the Big Wood River, the last remaining structure of Broadford Township has been saved and renovated. The solid sienna-colored log framework mellowed with time conjures images of harsh weather and high hopes of the early settlers. A series of three other structures added alongside the older log structure surpass previous builders' dreams.

Opposite: *With its integrity maintained, the original homestead house has a second story added as well as a major addition behind.*

Above: *Placement among treetops gives an immediate, magical sense of being elsewhere.*

Today, this is a family compound, built on a tradition of hospitality. Known for using clean lines and fine materials, designer-icon Ward Bennett melded a new addition to the rough-hewn cabin. With understatement and economy of design, the theme and integrity of basic materials cover everything from the log and chink to unadorned stainless steel, white wood panels, colorfully painted floors and industrial hardware. Well-chosen furnishings and a delicate balance of minimalism create a peaceful sophistication.

True to effectual design, new purpose is given to a stable. A fanciful conversion, it has three sleeping stalls and a separate bedroom stall. Original log ceiling beams, stall doors and barn hardware create a fun atmosphere and versatile interior.

Visitors experience the feeling of freedom in a guesthouse built upon concrete piers with a treetop lookout view. Interiors that reflect Shaker simplicity support Bennett's belief that elegant minimalism offset with industrial accents achieve a contemporary luxury, exuding peace and calm.

The pool house is an elegant reduction of elements with exquisite detailing. As pure and simple as the pool of water, all the surfaces reflect and repeat planarity. The simplicity is surprising and unpredictable with a refined sensibility reminiscent of sculpture. Peacefulness is the result of balance in the design. This retreat, first found by treasure seekers, reveals a later discovery of joy in family, friends and the tonic of open space. ✻

Rooflines and judicious choices of materials retain the homestead's original charm. The completed structure has a mature grace that never oversteps proper boundaries.

Opposite: Birds-eye views from the guest cottage on piers complete a comfortable nest of books and inviting seating arrangements.

Above: The master bedroom in the main house features collectible furniture and cleverly makes use of diagonal placements in design.

Below: Common items from different cultures, such as paper lanterns and a heavy plank harvest table, blend because of simplicity in design.

Opposite: The sparseness and use of stainless steel reflects the functional nature and economy of design.

Above: The use of industrial fixtures and simplistic design maintains tidiness.

Above: *Interior furnishings for the pool house are kept at the same minimal level as the overall design. Adornment is not needed.*

Below: *Just as a pause within a piece of music can add as much importance as the following notes, the restraint in design of the pool house creates a perfect composition. The architecture is an example of frozen music.*

Opposite: *When restoring the horse stable for a new purpose, knowing what not to change was more important than what to remodel.*

MORE IS NEVER
ENOUGH

S un Valley is a popular destination for families to gather for holidays and vacations. Many homes are shared for years by generations. In this home, a mother and daughter put their talents together to create this getaway with the motto, "More is never enough." Designed with one thousand and one impulses, they were not afraid to break rules and defy conventions, and the result is a delightful collection of rooms with clear expressions of personality. Putting together everything they loved, they created a perfect example of an eclectic style.

Tackling the look of profusion isn't for the fainthearted, but the two women mixed rather than matched the seriousness of antiques with the whimsy of collectibles. Exquisite sterling collections rest beside novelty salt-and-pepper shakers, and fine Parisian art hangs above monogrammed dog pillows. Every available surface is covered with keepsakes and shards of memories with fascinating stories to tell.

Above: Victorian screens extend an entry way, creating an unexpected backdrop within the living room.

Opposite: Warm dark woods, recessed lighting and fun yet functional furniture create a lavish kitchen space.

Although it only took four years, the home décor appears to be the accumulation of generations. Romance, nostalgia and originality team within these walls. A sense of luxury is underscored by superb detailing, such as fabrics that delight the eye—concoctions of silk, damask, brocades, ribbons, piping, tassels and trim cover beds, walls and frame windows. A multitude of patterns in pottery, porcelain, wallpaper, chintz and mementos combine into a vibrant elegance. ✳

Opposite: The bookcases in the library beckon to visitors to inspect their curious collections.

Above: Sentimental clutter that honors memories fills every flat space.

Below: Sensual silks and brocades of varying patterns are used on walls, headboards and pillows. Colors, style and the personality of the homeowner unite it all.

Above: *Proper lighting adds warmth and candles create romance.*

Below: *Tableaus created by gatherings of photos and treasures boldly reflect a sensibility of the sentimental.*

Opposite: *A witty mixing of French antique furniture with curious architectural pieces piques the imagination and maintains a lighthearted ambience.*

Above: *Unabashed girly trappings and feminine frills give this home a soft, comfortable atmosphere.*

Opposite: *The addition of mirrors to the bathroom walls increases the sense of space and brings in more light.*

Opposite: *An eclectic mix of potting urns and planters hint at the fun, unconventional decorating style inside.*

Above: *Good landscaping and placement of trees eliminates the need for a patio cover.*

Below: *The patio becomes a fantastic year-round outdoor room when "deep seating" furniture is used.*

TWINING OCCIDENTAL
& ORIENTAL

An antique iron gate and vintage screen door are the first objects to greet visitors to this home, which sits just twenty feet from Warm Springs Creek. The log construction is embellished with scalloped wood shingles, adding a storybook whimsy. Antique sculpture, native folk pieces and well-chosen odds and ends adorn the entry and porch, and hint at what surprises await inside.

A home is a sanctuary and this owner has established hers with sacred objects—a "calender" of saints abide alongside an eclectic mismatch of trappings. Within this character log home are crowded nesting areas filled with compulsive collections of the dissimilar. Here sacred and profane live together. The unrelated and visually at odds with each other reside crowded and bunched. It is a visual cacophony, but within the frenzy a consistency runs from room to room.

Opposite: A chair designed by Christian Liagre rests atop a vintage zebra-hide rug.

Above: Santos and saints create the feeling of an ever-occupied living room. The oversized mirror in an unexpected placement enlarges the apparent space, reflecting light endlessly.

The commonality of quality brings harmony to the décor. Furnishings and decorations are treated with the respect deserved of art. Choices made in collecting, combined with deliberate placement, give the chaos legitimacy. Surprise is added as the purpose, for many objects are reinvented. The discarded, forgotten, neglected, tattered and scarred are given recognition and honor. This home is filled with a self-confidence and one is commanded to examine it with new eyes.

There is a fearlessness and joy of life embraced in the décor. A shock of new perspective is the treasure found within this residence and an excitement in the passion of odd couplings. ☀

Above: Warm tones, sensuous shades and the power of mass combine to produce deliberate contrasts.

Opposite: Playful fabrics and whimsical furnishings make a teenage girl's bedroom a haven.

Above: *Objets d' art, oddities and the incongruous stimulate the imagination.*

Opposite: *Mismatched furnishings of period and style are twined together with confidence.*

Opposite: Beauty is in the eye of the beholder within this powder room and dressing table.

Above: Placed in their new home, the sacred and the profane live side by side.

Below: Displayed in a transitional area, a Ming dynasty robe chest and needlepoint Victorian chair provide space for storage and seating.

Above: *A delicate antique gate fits well with the rustic log construction.*

Below: *Scalloped shingles, chinked logs and an antique screen door mix texture and style, yet come together to create an inviting entry.*

Opposite: *Deliberate vintage choices in furnishings immerse the patio area into days gone by.*

AN AMERICAN
RETREAT

R eminiscent of a nineteenth-century sporting lodge, this rustic vacation home sits on a hilltop surrounded by forested acres. Occupied by a sports-oriented family, the structure provides a solid base for exploration and adventure.

With interiors of wide spaces and rooms with generous views, the house is as open as welcome arms. Winsome decoration and an extensive folk art collection live compatibly within the log walls. Well-chosen American antiques and vintage trade and advertising signs conjure images of family vacations with kids packed in the backseat, fits of fuss and wiggle until arrival. This home is meant for creating memories.

Pure space allows appreciation of the furniture, folk art and architectural details of the home. Game boards, canoes, regalia from outdoor sports and other common objects speak of plain family values and virtues, encouraging both adults and children to participate. Such an adventure-filled retreat is not just a location but a state of mind, and each visit adds memories in layers to the ones of the years before. Truly, it is an all-American theme exuding family fun. ✺

Above: Simple, natural vegetation is all the landscaping needed for this rustic lodge.

Opposite: Classic signs once seen on family road trips decorate the entrance.

Opposite: Expansive views and an open floor plan with exposed log-and-beam construction create the sporting lodge ambiance.

Above: An early hand-hooked rug from a fairytale classic hangs in the master bedroom. This wonderful folk-art piece of Goldilocks and the Three Bears is one of many museum-quality textile pieces displayed in the home.

Below: Letters gleaned from an old-fashioned advertisement sign spell out one of the family's best-loved activities.

Opposite: A custom-designed rug with the family's favorite activities complements the oversized couches covered in trout-patterned fabric. Antique country furnishings add warmth and character.

Above: A timeworn cupboard still functions in its original purpose—housing collectibles and everyday china.

Above: *Previously sitting atop a tourist motel in Iowa, this 1950s fiberglass cowboy on a rearing horse adds a touch of whimsy to the backyard meadow and national forest backdrop.*

Opposite: *Kitchen, dining and living rooms are separate but open, keeping things cozy.*

Opposite: *Memorabilia and carnival trinkets within add to the Western travel theme.*

Above: *Classic travel trailers stand as playful accommodations for guests.*

Below: *Restored interiors of trailers include novel materials such as discarded wine corks for paneling.*

OLD - WORLD
SOPHISTICATION

H alf-hidden behind wooded berms, a European hunting lodge rests in the bucolic Idaho riverside. Inside, a time-less air reigns over polished furniture, rich wood paneling, heavy beams accented with carved rams head corbels, comforting chairs and rooms that echo conversations of travel and politics. Often filled with the fragrance of newly cut greens, flowers, wood smoke and buffed table tops, the home invites one to curl up with a classic book, attempt a new bread recipe, or sketch.

The feeling of old Europe can be experienced immediately upon entering the grand foyer. Architect James Ruscitto and the owners scoured the salvage yards of France and Belgium to gather doors, beams, fireplace mantels, paneling and other architectural elements to perfect this design. The wood and stone floors and the restored open-timbered ceiling add a real sense of age. Hunting trophies from far-off lands hang on the walls, adding atmosphere as well as decoration.

Opposite: *Antique European doors receive dramatic architectural framing.*

Above: *Natural stone set into grass harmonizes with the stone construction of the home.*

The stone-paved corridor into the living room seems to lead to another century—one of luxurious comfort and charmed elegance. Heavily cushioned and pillowed window seats create separate areas within the larger living space. Careful choices of decorations add a worldly stateliness and avoid the trendy. Small clusters of objects reveal the owners' interests—pottery, antiques, and photographs of dignitaries, presidential candidates and family.

Although the home's tranquil atmosphere references the past, it has been designed for today's living yet is independent of passing fashion. Homes do resemble their inhabitants, and this one displays originality and imagination rather than convention. ✹

Above: *More than sixty tons of lumber, paneling and doors were imported from Belgium to achieve the aged look.*

Opposite: *A massive coffee table matches the scale of the room, allowing for various seating arrangements around it.*

Above: *A buffet stores china. The doors have been re-hung and reversed to stay open for display.*

Opposite: *A carved antique wood fireplace imported from Belgium dominates the library.*

Above: Framed mirrors on both walls increase the light and size of the powder room.

Below: Native American sculpture, pottery and Meso-American sculpture speak of extensive travel.

Opposite: Both practical and charming, French butcher blocks are incorporated into the kitchen. The warm color of wood, stone and terra-cotta tiles rest in harmony.

Opposite: *Collectibles, books and family photography fill the library shelves to capacity, and invite one to explore them in depth.*

Above: *Antique silver with elk and pheasant motifs evoke half-remembered memories of a bygone era.*

Below: *A massive stone bas-relief of a lion and lamb found in a French architectural salvage yard stands guard in the foyer.*

ROCKING T
RANCH

At first, the property seems devoid of human owners. Dogs wag their greeting and two portly miniature horses purchased at a garage sale can be seen, ruling the corrals, huffing, kicking dirt and making demands. The red barn is home to these and more, and at first seems to be the only structure in sight. However, matching the barn is a storybook cottage with a whimsical arched front door covered by cascading roofs. These are inviting buildings, offering refuge far from the cacophony of city life.

Landscaping was designed with the mercurial climate in mind, so gardens were planted natural and loose and flowerbeds were cultivated with enthusiastic experimentation and abandon. Hearty vines climb up posts and over patio lattice covers. Surrounding the house are aspen, spruce, pine and alpine shrubbery, herbage, greens and flora that thrive here naturally.

Above: Although the landscaping appears spontaneous, it is a result of years of experimentation with perennials.

Opposite: Back patio trellises overflow with vines as outdoor furniture is arranged in intimate settings for friends and family.

Collections of oddities populate the apartment over the garage. It is filled and decorated with treasures gleaned from flea markets, auctions, garage sales and alleyways the night before trash pickup. Objects discarded in silent dark places find newly recognized worth once spotted by a gifted eye. There is a tranquil relief in the curious tableaus and respect for the integrity of things whose beauty was bestowed by hand and by age.

The appeal of this cottage is that it projects a mix of classic styles, with small rooms snugly packed in perfect scale. Rich fabrics present posh and pampered atmosphere, while tables display Asian figurines and foo dogs tangled in crawling ivy next to French lamps. Ignoring convention, the unrelated or conflicting are put together, and just like a happy ending, their style differences are settled and peace is made. ☀

Opposite: *Horses and dogs are an integral part of life here.*

Above: *Rooflines trimmed in heavy molding frame a cottage home whimsical in character and generous in spirit.*

Above: *The small but well-planned rooms remind one of an English cottage.*

Below: *No matter what objects make up a collection, the whole must be interesting and pleasing to the eye.*

Opposite: *Without borrowing a particular style but embracing substance, the owner has created a home with heart, not just surface pleasures.*

Opposite: *A fanciful tableau of architectural elements and found objects creates a bold room divider.*

Above: *Treasures clustered together become an interesting display.*

Opposite: Without looking over her shoulder for approval, the owner put together this room as a sanctuary and retreat from the world.

Above: The celebration of familiar objects are complete in their imperfection and age.

Below: Indoor and outdoor furniture set on the lawn create a whole new room outdoors.

HISTORIC CABIN ON
TRAIL CREEK

This weather-beaten cabin located on the edge of Trail Creek possesses a soul. Built as a fishing cottage in 1915, the cozy space was frequently rented out to tourists during summers. One visitor arrived in 1943—a naval psychiatrist stationed at Sun Valley Lodge. At that time the lodge had been commissioned as a naval convalescent hospital, and for the next couple of years, more than 7,000 patients were treated there. After the war, the doctor purchased the cabin and added a living room and bedroom in 1954 to accommodate an expanding family and its vacations.

Western and rustic style is often loved to death, with its integrity corroded by clichés like ceramic buffaloes and rubber tomahawks. That is not for the residents of this rustic cabin, who take delight in showcasing the mundane along with traditional Adirondack and classic cowboy style. These avid collectors scour flea markets and secondhand stores to gather tarnished and overlooked objects in order to display them here. Ordinary objects are made extraordinary by these rustic-style aficionados, who are passionate about the unconventional.

Opposite: Treasures hunted down in various odd places become hard to part with.

Above: The garden shed was remodeled into a cozy guest room adorned with vigorous vines, architectural discards and overlooked treasures.

This compact shelter is filled with curious textures and colors mixed together to reveal the layered characteristics of the occupants. In a style that could be described as creative chaos, this inviting home is truly a work of the imagination. Nevertheless, residents in this pocket-sized paradise still appreciate the simplicity of life that this one-time fishing cabin offers. ✳

Above: *Informal groupings of family photos reveal both the cabin's and family's history—and it is impossible to separate the two.*

Opposite: *With quirky flair, the owners demonstrate an appreciation for humble elegance and a love of comfort in the bedroom.*

Opposite: The kitchen area provides a feast for all the senses.

Above: Once all flat surfaces are covered, keepsakes move to adorn the walls.

Below: Many of the objects that decorate the home were carefully selected from thrift stores and flea markets, and each piece stands alone as an interesting collectible.

The rough stone fireplace is more than enough to warm this tiny haven. It's easy to imagine cold, wet fishermen thawing out after a day in the nearby river.

Scarred and battered, the front door shows its age with signs of happy comings and goings.

Above: *Trail Creek provides the occupants of the cabin with many things—a lovely view, restful sounds and the occasional meal.*

Below: *An old wagon once filled with mining supplies now finds new purpose in the landscape.*

Opposite: *A mix of wild nature and found objects mesh the natural and man-made into a delightful patio area.*

A CIVILIZED
SECLUSION

Just as a different language can restructure a new way of interpreting life's experiences, a change of culture can refresh and inspire. Away from the predictable, new terrains alter the pace and metabolism of life. The vacation home is a place to unwind, indulge in a favorite sport and develop new perspectives.

This great escape was originally a bed-and-breakfast lodge. Architect James Ruscitto's task was to transform a commercial property into a residential family getaway while creating curb appeal in the process. With good "bones" and the overall purpose of the building remaining the same, relatively minimal structural remodeling was required; adding a new garage and expansions above the old one gave new scale to the residence. Deriving structure from nature, Ruscitto wrapped the entire base of the house in river rock, blending the residence with the mountain behind.

Above: *Window boxes provide abundant foliage for even a small deck.*

Opposite: *The new owners of this former bed-and-breakfast inn moved the main entrance from the street view to the side.*

The original entry to the inn has been transformed into a living room with window space for expansive views and natural light. A bold stone stairway was added as the new entrance with a massive door opening to the new foyer. Handsome warm walls of hand-tooled leather allow a better sense of arrival with pause and drama. The former lodge now contains two living rooms with twelve bedrooms set along hallways that run the length of the home, and each room has a balcony with mountain views. The kitchen, once responsible for feeding a multitude of guests, was updated to professional standards with state-of-the-art equipment, providing a suitable workplace for the finest chefs, yet comfortable enough to prepare a cozy family meal.

A uniting palette of warm earth tones with accents of crimson and leafy greens is repeated throughout the warp of fabrics, rugs, extensive collections of museum-quality Native American basketry and beadwork. Clever use is made of rustic decorative arts from many cultures, including Western, such as objects from the French countryside, Tuscany and rural China. With its comfortable mix of rustic and refined, this home's style is sometimes unexpected but always elegant. ✸

Opposite: *Because of the structure's previous role as an inn, all the bedrooms have private patios.*

Above: *Walls painted in a warm palette and soft lighting make a peaceful setting for collections of primitives, including Plains Indian beaded blanket strips and moccasins.*

Above: Blends of French antiques, American folk art and rustic architecture form an easy warmth.

Below: Rich wood tones, soft celadon walls and romantic sconces create a natural palette in this rustic home's powder room.

Opposite: Ample and comfortable seating sits amidst fir ceilings and exposed rafters to develop a warm, natural haven.

Opposite: In a combination family room/office/media room, oversized armchairs and ottomans sport faux tiger skin fabric, and a contemporary black leather sofa sets the tone for a relaxed multi-use environment.

Above: Prominently displayed is an antique Sioux beaded vest.

Opposite: *Reclaimed space is found under a stairway, creating a cozy seating area. Pueblo pottery, Native American baskets and leather chairs with a Chinese trunk in between are a compatible blend of rich textures and tones.*

Above: *In the upstairs den, a custom cabinet with built-in lights houses a major collection of Plains Indian dolls, moccasins, beaded bags and miniature cradles.*

Below: *Woods, reeds, textures and different shades of timber unify the interior. Quality is the common foundation of grace and style in this home.*

NATURE AND
NURTURE

T homas Jefferson remarked that "no occupation is so delightful as the culture of the earth and no culture comparable to that of the garden." The most imaginative gardens usually belong to those with an artistic streak, and they act as a means of expression. Nature and nurture combine through labor and love and the enjoyment of its rewards are worth every hour.

Sun Valley's climate can be dramatic and harsh, and coaxing a garden here is always a challenge. Defying all odds, this garden is a flourishing oasis of calm and serenity due to the owner's dedication and loyalty in pursuing its cultivation. This gardener's secret of success is her kinship with life. A river borders her eight acres, which are part of the natural passage of elk and deer. Consideration and respectful stewardship of the property is mandatory. A unique symbiosis occurs on this land—twisted queues of espaliered apple trees are planted in sufficient abundance to accommodate "nibbling" and the elk prune the tender shoots. Ladybugs and praying mantis are pitted against aphids as natural protection, giving regard to the vulnerabilities of birds and a pet pug.

Opposite: The garden is not merely a plot for growing plants but is an integral part of the home, a room without walls. Architectural pieces punctuate the décor.

Above: Waiting for flowers to bloom allows the gardener time to appreciate the seasons.

The garden is a series of visual surprises. Water is used as an ornament enhancing color, relieving the extensive open spaces and serving to emphasize the shifts between levels. Downhill streams and connecting pools add rich and refreshing sounds. By varying the schemes, the composition avoids the predictable. The owner's artistic whims and horticultural passions add irregular touches infused with energy: trained clematis climb fruit trees, rock plants tuck snugly into crevices between stones and collections of succulents grow from moss balls that hang from ornamental trees. What may appear spontaneous and casual is carefree only to the eye.

Ensuring a synchronized display of coinciding blooms or coordinated dimensions and proportions requires experience and knowledge. Lush shoots and arching sprays live in profusion beside broad varieties of flowers and perennial borders planted in tiers. A fancier version of the English garden—mixed borders, bridal arches, kitchen gardens—the owner integrated all the most admired elements into her landscaping. A classic, raised kitchen garden is the only protected area, with sides of decorative wrought iron cloaked and embellished with climbing vines. Champagne grapes spill over a back wall onto paths bordered by salad greens growing in low rows. Elsewhere tomatoes are decoratively staked and green beans climb trellises next to shallots, leeks, potatoes, herbs and flowers for cutting. Baskets of flowers and vegetables picked daily emphasize a lifestyle close to the earth and harmonious with its bounty. ✴

Beyond the antique gate, a profusion of flowers entwine in a riot of multi-colored blooms in all shades.

Opposite: *Architectural salvage pieces blend with stone steps, repeating materials used within the house.*

Above: *Succulents grown in balls of moss create a sculptural effect.*

Below: *Wells and cisterns were used in gardens before water hoses made their appearance. A detail such as plumbing a Celtic well to produce refreshing water sounds adds to the aging process of this garden.*

Opposite: *Stone globes at the pond's edge serve as focal points, giving a sense of balance and structure to the outdoor space.*

Above: *The greenhouse off the kitchen creates a livable space, combining the best features of indoors and out.*

Above: The kitchen garden is the only one gated to protect it from animals.

Below: A pond sits among barely-tamed flowers and vines, providing a tranquil water element.

Opposite: Plant life enhances the stone entrance structure with vines clinging to walls and trees curving inward toward the roofline.

TERRITORIAL
HOMESTEAD

Owner and architect Austen T. Gray's intent was to create a home reminiscent of an original Old West homestead. His roots and passion were in territorial architecture (a tradition originating from the East Coast). It was the official style designated by Washington, D.C., for forts and government buildings in the West. The work of architect Jonathan Foote and his use of hand-hewn beams, barn timber and native stone also provided inspiration.

Placement, manner and bearings of the buildings evoke the romance of an early homestead, with the main residence in the center and other more modest buildings surrounding it. On this property, the bunkhouse (or guesthouse), built of hundred-year-old barn wood, is separated and off to one side of the main ranch house.

Above: The bunkhouse, a separate building, provides guest quarters for family and friends. The cupola allows extra height and light into the sitting room.

Opposite: One hundred-year-old salvaged board is used as siding with exposed joints and connections. The architect's trademark cupola and weather vane top the barn, which serves as the garage and upstairs game room.

Educated at Harvard and in Idaho, Gray remembers his early fascination with the farms in the fertile Palouse area of eastern Washington and northwestern Idaho. It is an area of unique beauty, of undulating hills and rich farmland dotted with clusters of trees. He incorporated the Scandinavian construction design found throughout this region in his design. At the apex of the roofs, he uses the decorative outrigger beams for support. Cupolas, Eastern in origin and embraced as a personal trademark, are put on each of his designs, and he finds they are a good excuse to have a weather vane. The cupola on the barn has a clock, as if to remind cowhands of chores to be done.

In the main house, all rooms were designed with generous views of Big Wood River. Windows at each end catch the early morning sun, and red foxes and rogue male moose often take up residence on the grass lawn. In recent years, a family of elk has begun to frequent the common picnic area. The home is a visual narrative of romanticized times when gutsy Americans, armed with determination and fortitude, claimed land and built futures. The fruits of labor and serenity of success reside here. ✳

Opposite: *The symmetrical entry was designed to create privacy. The driveway has a snow-melt system to keep it clear during the winter.*

Above: *A freestanding fireplace and wicker furnishings create an outdoor room with views of the river. Herbs grow between stones and are watered hydroponically.*

Above: Earth tones and rustic textures are used with oversized furniture, and patterns and themes of a Western ranch house repeat throughout to provide frontier informality.

Opposite: A 1930s metal Pontiac weather vane sits upon the hand-hewn mantel. The oversized scale adds the excitement associated with frontier life.

Above: A sculpture in its own right, this Victorian rancher's rack of hoof and horn holding a lasso and cowboy hats are part of the home's rough-and-ready style.

Below: Native American-like geometric patterns are included in the tile design, repeating the theme throughout the house.

Opposite: Kitchen construction included reclaimed wood, with windows reminiscent of an old homestead.

Opposite: Adjacent to the kitchen, a seating area with oversized armchairs, a vintage twig rocker and custom-made rag rug reflects an all-American warmth.

Above: A feminine bedroom adorned with floral patterns blends well with an animal print bedspread.

Below: A rustic Chinese drum serves as a table in front of a tumbled tile-mosaic fireplace. A vintage 1930 Western movie poster rests on the hand-hewn mantel.

A R T F U L
SANCTUARY

ural in setting but sophisticated in execution, this residence is a compilation of cherished art and objects. With seven interconnected structures totaling 19,000 square feet, it is a unique place for viewing a continuous flow of art. The home houses a collection of 650 artworks such as paintings, photography, sculptures, vintage Thomas Molesworth furniture and antiques. The owners desired form to follow function, and wanted a home created that

sat in harmony with its natural surroundings. With restraining touch and carefully placed elements that do not detract from the richness of trees, sky and water, architect Frederick Fisher of Los Angeles, California, achieved this balance.

The embracing of all things creative is evident in the 1,000-square-foot kitchen. It includes three work islands, a pizza oven, a rotisserie, multiple stoves, walk-in refrigerators and a wine cellar.

Elsewhere within the residence is a landscaped courtyard, where an elegant transition occurs from the courtyard to an open 1,100-square-foot gallery. As part of the interconnected structures, two 25-foot-tall galvanized-steel silo containers house bedroom suites. The farm image fits comfortably with exterior siding made of recycled fir gleaned from abandoned mining structures. ☀

Opposite: *Sliding pocket doors open to a landscaped courtyard designed by Kelley Weston and the reflecting fountain created by Meg Webster.*

Above: *An arched portico marks the entrance to the compound.*

Above: *Paintings by Marilyn Minter hang in an oversized breakfast nook off the kitchen.*

Below: *Collections are a passion to the owners of this home. French lunch boxes sit together, a multitude of color and texture within a single shape.*

Opposite: *Surrounding a custom table with a built-in lazy Susan are vintage Molesworth chairs. A gathering of sculpture and art, including mercury glass candlesticks, surround the room.*

Opposite: *The fireplace supports a massive stone mantle. The grand room is made cozy with the use of oversized leather couches, Navajo rugs and a stylized coffee table.*

Above: *The art of Jerry Kearns hangs over a Molesworth bed, evoking a tongue-in-cheek Western masculinity.*

Below: *Salvaged from the George Summers "Old Lodge" in Glenwood Springs (circa 1935), this original Thomas Molesworth red-painted wrought-iron mounted pine door opens into an office. The door interior is decorated with Native American–inspired hieroglyphs.*

Opposite: *The gallery accommodates the scale of sculpture and displays "Cup Kids," the work of artist Yoshitoma Nara.*

Above: *Guest suites are housed within galvanized steel silos, part of a series of interconnected blocks.*

Above: *A collection of carnival chalkware figurines sits on an office book-case. A Molesworth armchair and a burlwood side table are positioned in front.*

Below: *Water flows over an exterior wall of flat-stacked rocks to be recirculated back to the rooftop lap pool and spa. Repeating the textural lines of the backdrop wall, a sculpture by Antony Gormley Domain XV (2000) stands mid-step.*

Opposite: *Open doors provide an exciting visual flow from the bar through the courtyard to the gallery. A collection of photographs from Robert Frank's book The Americas (1956) resides here.*

M O U N T A I N
MINIMALISM

S tepping into this elegantly edited house is like walking into a sculpture with doorways and windows. The 6,000-square-foot vacation home provides a sophisticated and serene year-round retreat for its New York owners. The fir-sided, steel-framed and poured-in-place concrete structure is complemented by aluminum fenestration throughout and frames the stunning landscape.

The purity of the structure is maintained by sparseness, and there is a hint of Japanese influence in its art of restraint and nuance. By keeping the walls open and clear, the space appears expanded, allowing the room to breathe. This design was a matter of subtraction rather than addition, and the reduction of style to a few good pieces surrounded by space creates a greater impact.

Above: The simple design is gem-like in the winter evenings.

Opposite: From the inside, the windows act like frames, enclosing spectacular and carefully chosen views.

Recessed halo lights are used throughout the living and dining room ceilings, where they appear as starry constellations when seen from the street at night. Seemingly random, each light was placed with specific purpose and wattage for its use—to highlight art, add drama to the fireplace or enhance dining.

The kitchen is a collage of color, space and surface quality. Cabinets of birch covered with tinted acrylic panels coordinate with colors, patterns and textures, creating a soothing alliance of design. A solar-shade drop screen separates the kitchen from the rest of the house as needed, allowing a more formal presence. Banks of voluminous windows flank the dining room displaying the grandeur of mountain views. Designed with flowing space, the residence reflects the openness of the West. ✹

Opposite: A pale palette with green and red accents gives a sense of space and continuity.

Above: Space was deliberately designed for displaying art. Sliding walls in the living room take the place of doors.

Opposite: *Balance, lighting and clever use of materials make the atmosphere warm.*

Above: *Celadon acrylic wall panels with a brushed aluminum railing flank stairs of birch. Frosted glass is used on the stairwell—a surprisingly successful example of common materials used for uncommon purposes.*

Above: *Drama in design is achieved by allowing air space between the stairs and walls.*

Below: *The oversized front door is hinged approximately one-third of the way in to save space.*

Opposite: *Exterior views and uncluttered interiors allow the architecture to stand on its own without excessive adornment.*

Opposite: *Clean lines and well-planned spacing based on human actions and needs produce an efficient kitchen and purposeful design.*

Above: *Illuminated acrylic panels create magical surfaces.*

Below: *Birch cabinets support a sink of whimsical proportions.*

Above: Exterior construction is kept as minimal in design as the interior.

Opposite: The upstairs patio is a continuation of the interior design's simplicity and emphasis upon views.

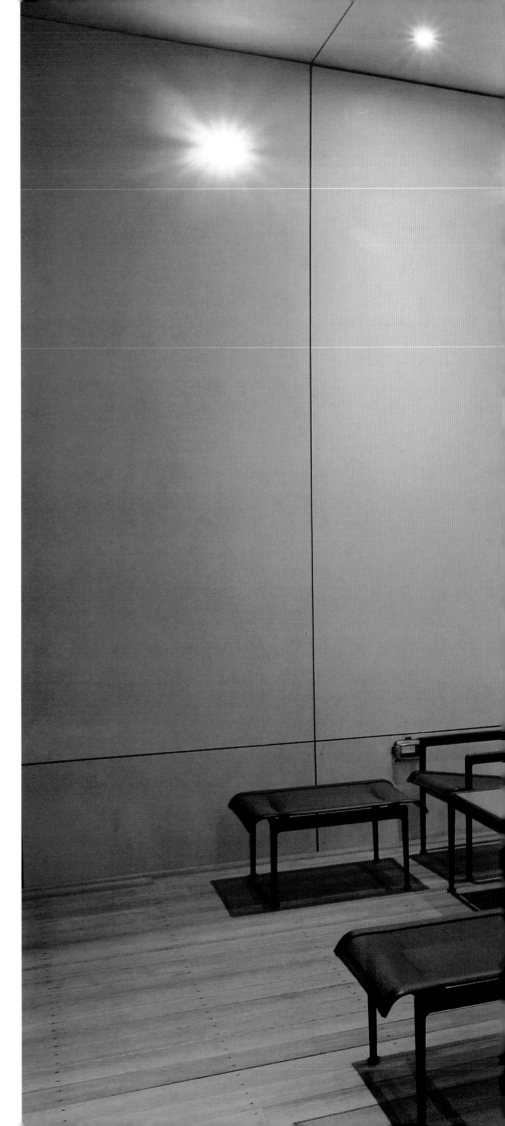

CREDITS

PHOTOGRAPHY CREDITS

All photos courtesy of Tim Brown (208-726-6615) with the following exceptions:

Alan Edison, American West Gallery Collection: pg. 9, 10 (upper left), 13, 15, 16, 19, 22, 24, 26, 28 (upper left)

Michael Engl Collection: pg. 10 (lower right), 14, 18, 20, 21, 27, (upper left), 29, 31 ,32, 33

Vickey Hanson, Mountain Dream Works: pg. 8, 17, 23, 27 (lower right)

Adam Turtletaub Collection: pg. 11, 28 (lower left), 30

Saul and Shirley Turtletaub Collection: pg. 25

Richard and Susan Watkins: pg. 12

HOMES AND LANDSCAPING

NATURE OF RESTRAINT

Architect:
Michael Doty, AIA
Michael Doty Associates Architects
P.O. Box 2792
371 Washington Avenue North
Ketchum, Idaho 83340
208-726-4228 phone
208-726-4188 fax
www.mda-arc.com

Contractor:
Adam Elias
Elias Construction
P.O. Box 6272
131 4th Street, Suite 211
Ketchum, Idaho 83340
208-725-5400 phone
208-725-5402 fax

Interior Designer:
Jonathan Staub
Your Space Interiors
643 Seventh Street
San Francisco, California 94103
415-565-6767 phone
415-565-6701 fax
www.your-space.com

Landscape Architect:
Bruce D. Hinckley
Alchemie
P.O. Box 604
Sun Valley, Idaho 83353
208-726-3256 phone
208-521-0358 fax
www.alchemiesites.com

Lighting Designer:
Paul Stoops, PE
P.O. Box 1130
Hailey, Idaho 83333
208-788-8993 phone
208-788-7634 fax

Media Consultant:
Kevin Carey
Home Media
111 Lewis Street
Ketchum, Idaho 83340
208-725-0075 phone
208-725-0391 fax
www.homemedia.net

ART AND ARCHITECTURE

Architect:
Janet Jarvis, AIA
Jarvis Group Architects
511 Sun Valley Road
P.O. Box 626
Ketchum, Idaho 83340
208-726-4031 phone
208-726-4097 fax
www.jarvis-group.com

Nandinee Phookan Architect
Design Architect: Caitlan Moore
108 Wooster Street, #C2
New York, New York 10012
212-226-1500 phone
212-226-7547 fax
www.nandineephookan.com

Contractor:
Engelmann
Project Manager: Alan Gelet
Superintendent on-site: Ben Berntson
Superintendent on-site: Scott Stevenson
660 - 2nd Avenue South
P.O. Box 6240
Ketchum, Idaho 83340
208-726-9742 phone
www.engelmann-inc.com

Interior Designer:
Nandinee Phookan Architect
Interior Designer: Caitlan Moore
108 Wooster Street #C2
New York, New York 10012
212-226-1500 phone
212-226-7547 fax
www.nandineephookan.com

Landscape Designer:
All Season's Landscaping
901 South Main Street
Bellevue, Idaho 83313
208-788-3352 phone

LESS IS A LOT MORE WORK
Architect:
Susan Desko, AIA
P.O. Box 6496
Ketchum, Idaho 83340
208-726-0155 phone
sdesko@susandesko-aia.com

Contractor:
Kearns Builders, Inc.
P.O. Box 3233
Ketchum, Idaho 83340
208-726-4843 phone
www.kearnsbuilders.com

Interior Designer:
Jill Vogel Interiors

Landscape Designer:
Jim Freeman Landscaping
P.O. Box 1860
Ketchum, Idaho 83340-1860
208-726-1936 phone

RIVER RETREAT
Architect:
Serena Stewart
New York, New York
Contractor:
Richard Fabiano Construction
P.O. Box 4929
Ketchum, Idaho 83340
208-720-1423 phone

Interior Designer:
Charles Stuhlberg, Inc.
Stuhlbergs Furniture—Interior Design
511 East Avenue North
Ketchum, Idaho 83340
208-726-4568 phone

P.O. Box 629
Sun Valley, Idaho 83353

Landscape Designer:
Owner

TRUE WEST
Architect:
Oregon Log Home Company
Project Manager: Bill Neary
P.O. Box 310
1399 North Highway 197
Maupin, Oregon 97037
541-395-2533 phone
www.oregonloghomes.com

Contractor:
Dembergh Construction, Inc.
Project Manager: Eric Grossbaum
111 West 6th Street
P.O. Box 3006
Ketchum, Idaho 83340
208-726-2440 phone
726-2440-2443 fax
info@dembergh.com
www.dembergh.com

Interior Designer:
Owner

Landscape Designer:
Webb Landscape, Inc.
891 Washington Avenue
Ketchum, Idaho 83340
208-726-7213 phone
www.webbland.com

TIMELESS HOMESTEAD
Architects:
Wright, Bryant & Johnson Inc., AIA
Project Architect: Woodrow Bryant, AIA
600 First Avenue North
Ketchum, Idaho 83340

P.O. Box 21
Sun Valley, Idaho 83353
208-726-4434 phone
208-726-8413 fax
www.wbjarchitects.com

Lake/Flato Architects, Inc.
311 Third Street, Suite 200
San Antonio, Texas 78205
210-227-3335 phone
210-224-9515 fax
www.lakeflato.com

Architect: Pool House
Lake/Flato Architects, Inc.
311 Third Street, Suite 200
San Antonio, Texas 78205
210-227-3335 phone
210-224-9515 fax
www.lakeflato.com

Architect: Guesthouse & Remodel
Wright, Bryant & Johnson Inc., AIA
Project Architect: Woodrow Bryant, AIA
600 First Avenue North
Ketchum, Idaho 83340

P.O. Box 21
Sun Valley, Idaho 83353
208-726-4434 phone
208-726-8413 fax
www.wbjarchitects.com

Interior Designer:
Ward Bennett, ASID
New York, New York

Contractor:
Jerry Broadie
Broadie Construction
Bellevue, Idaho 83313
208-788-2822 phone

Bishop Builders, Inc.
128 Saddle Road, Suite 104
P.O. Box 1746
Ketchum, Idaho 83340
208-726-9717 phone

Landscape Designer:
Matt Nye
New York, New York

MORE IS NEVER ENOUGH
Architect:
Clay Pereira
4199 Campus Drive
Irvine, California 92612

Contractor:
Roth Construction Company
P.O. Box 2040
Sun Valley, Idaho 83353

Interior Designers:
Janie Bolton
3208 West McGraw
Seattle, Washington 98199
206-284-2407 phone

Jani Poole
3858 - 31st Avenue West
Seattle, Washington 98199
206-283-8145 phone

Kirk Pereira
Pereira Designe
8132 West 4th Street
Los Angeles, California 90048

Landscape Designer:
Joe Hitzel

TWINING OCCIDENTAL AND ORIENTAL
Interior Designer:
Annette Frehling
P.O. Box 6486
Ketchum, Idaho 83340
sisterinketchum@aol.com

Landscape Designer:
Annette Frehling
P.O. Box 6486
Ketchum, Idaho 83340
sisterinketchum@aol.com

AN AMERICAN RETREAT

Architect:
Helen Ziegler
113 Abby Road
Hailey, Idaho 83333
208-788-4657 phone

Contractor:
Tom Ziegler
113 Abby Road
Hailey, Idaho 83333
208-788-4657 phone

Interior Designer:
Owner
Diamond Baratta Design
William Diamond
Anthony Baratta
270 Lafayette Street, Suite 1501
New York, New York 10012
212-966-8892 phone

Landscape Designer:
Karen Keiski
Stanley, Idaho

OLD WORLD SOPHISTICATION

Architect:
James Ruscitto, AIA
Ruscitto-Latham-Blanton Architectura
711 Washington Avenue North
P.O. Box 419
Sun Valley, Idaho 83353
208-726-5608 phone
208-726-1033 fax
www.rlb-sv.com

Contractor:
Wilson Construction
251 Northwood Way, Suite F
P.O. Box 6770
Ketchum, Idaho 83340
208-726-9776 phone

Interior Designer:
Owners

James Ruscitto, AIA
Ruscitto-Latham-Blanton Architectura
711 Washington Avenue North
P.O. Box 419
Sun Valley, Idaho 83353
208-726-5608 phone
208-726-1033 fax
www.rlb-sv.com

Landscape Designer:
Webb Landscape, Inc.
162 Glendale Road
Bellevue, Idaho 83313
208-788-2066
www.webbland.com

ROCKING T RANCH

Architect:
James Ruscitto, AIA
Ruscitto-Latham-Blanton Architectura
711 Washington Avenue North
P.O. Box 419
Sun Valley, Idaho 83353
208-726-5608 phone
208-726-1033 fax
www.rlb-sv.com

Contractor:
Stephen Housel
Housel Construction
P.O. Box 445
Ketchum, Idaho 83340
208-578-2222 phone

Interior Designer:
Carol Thielen
Antiquities
440 East Avenue North
P.O. Box 6056
Ketchum, Idaho 83340
208-622-4577 phone
Landscape Designer:
Owner

Floral Designer:
Kurt McAuley
Botanica
331 - 1st Avenue North
Ketchum, Idaho 83340
208-725-2229 phone

A CIVILIZED SECLUSION

Architect:
James Ruscitto, AIA
Ruscitto-Latham-Blanton Architectura
711 Washington Avenue North
P.O. Box 419
Sun Valley, Idaho 83353
208-726-5608 phone
208-726-1033 fax
www.rlb-sv.com

Contractor:
Storey Construction, Inc.
323 Lewis Street, Suite L
P.O. Box 1877
Ketchum, Idaho 83340
208-726-8816 phone
208-726-2180 fax
www.storeyconstruction.com

Interior Designer
ACP Home
Owner Designer: Elizabeth Jones
P.O. Box 6369
340 Walnut Ave.
Ketchum, Idaho 83340
208-622-7551 phone
208-622-8007 fax
elizabeth@acphome.com
www.acphome.com

Landscape Architect:
Steven A. Job, ASLA
180 - 7th Street East, Suite 1A
Ketchum, Idaho 83340
208-726-3887 phone

NATURE AND NURTURE

Architect:
James Ruscitto, AIA
Ruscitto-Latham-Blanton Architectura
711 Washington Avenue North
P.O. Box 419
Sun Valley, Idaho 83353
208-726-5608 phone
208-726-1033 fax
www.rlb-sv.com

TERRITORIAL HOMESTEAD

Architect:
Austen T. Gray
A. T. Architect, PC
111 Piping Rock Road
Locust Valley, New York 11560
516-671-3267 phone
516-671-3539 fax

Contractor:
Dembergh Construction, Inc.
Principal: Peter Dembergh
Project Manager: Ken Ferris
111 West 6th Street
P.O. Box 3006
Ketchum, Idaho 83340
208-726-2440 phone
726-2440-2443 fax
info@dembergh.com
www.dembergh.com

Interior Designer:
Lone Star Designs
Owner Designer: Terri DeMunn
P.O. Box 698
109 South Main Street
Hailey, Idaho 83333
208-788-9158 phone
208-788-9170 fax

Landscape Architect:
Eggers Associates
Kurt Eggers
P.O. Box 953
1007 Warm Springs Road #G
Ketchum, Idaho 83340
208-725-0988 phone
208-725-0972 fax

ARTFUL SANCTUARY

Architect:
Frederick Fisher and Partners Architects
12248 Santa Monica Boulevard
Los Angeles, California 90025-2518
310-820-6680 phone
310-820-6118 fax
www.fisherpartners.net

Contractor:
Storey Construction, Inc.
323 Lewis Street, Suite L
P.O. Box 1877
Ketchum, Idaho 83340
208-726-8816 phone
208-726-2180 fax
www.storeyconstruction.com

Interior Designer:
Linda Marder Interior Design
8835 Wonderland Avenue
Los Angeles, California 90046-1851
323-656-8844 phone
323-656-0422 fax

Landscape Designer:
Kelley Weston
Native Landscapes
117 Blackfeet Drive
P.O. Box 4012
Hailey, Idaho 83333
208-578-2200 phone
208-578-2274 fax
www.coolnativelandscapes.com

Lighting Designer:
Andrew Schloss
ABS Design
347 West 22nd Street #5
New York, New York 10011
212-691-9622 phone
917-885-8125 cell

Furniture Designer:
Roy McMakin, Inc.
Domestic Architecture
Big Leaf Manufacturing Co.
Domestic Furniture Work Shop
1422 - 34th Avenue
Seattle, Washington 98122
206-323-0111 phone

Media Consultant:
Rich La Monico
20732 Dolorosa Street
Woodland Hills, California 91367
818-887-1670 phone
818-704-1949 fax

MOUNTAIN MINIMALISM
Architect:
SPG Architects
Partner in Charge: Coty Sidnam
Project Team: Coty Sidnam
Project Team: William Petrone
136 West 21 Street
New York, New York 10011
212-366-5500 phone
www.spgarchitects.com

Contractor:
Engelmann Inc.
Project Manager: Alan Gelet
Superintendent on-site: Ben Berntson
Superintendent on-site:
Scott Stevenson
660 - 2nd Avenue South
P.O. Box 6240
Ketchum, Idaho 83340
208-726-9742 phone
www.engelmann-inc.com

Interior Designer:
Owner

SPG Architects
Partner in Charge: Coty Sidnam
Project Team: Coty Sidnam
Project Team: William Petrone
136 West 21 Street
New York, New York 10011
212-366-5500 phone
www.spgarchitects.com

Landscape Designer:
All Season's Landscaping
901 South Main Street
Bellevue, Idaho 83313
208-788-3352 phone

ACKNOWLEDGMENTS

ALAN EDISON

My life changed forever when I took my first trip to Idaho more than sixteen years ago. My lovely wife, now lovely ex-wife, and I had always taken an annual winter ski trip to Colorado since it was a relatively easy trip from our home in Chicago. One year, we wanted to do something more adventurous, so we decided to check out the faraway wilderness of Sun Valley, Idaho, and see what America's first all-season, world-class resort was all about.

Like most people, I associated Idaho with its most famous export—the potato. As everyone knows, there are millions of them all over the place. My second association was with one of my favorite authors—sportsman and raconteur, the late and prolific Ernest Hemingway. In a nutshell, that was the sum total of my knowledge about Idaho.

Our adventure began when we flew from O'Hare into Boise and rented a car for the two-hour trip to Sun Valley. I was immediately impressed with the wide-open spaces, lack of billboards, and gently rolling hills as we drove east up into the mountains.

By the time we hit the town of Bellevue, I was growing concerned. As we drove through Hailey, I was fully worried. Although the town was perfectly charming with its historic buildings and low-key ambiance, I was totally unimpressed with the silhouette of the dark hills that led to the town of Ketchum. At the time, it all seemed very foreboding and not particularly welcoming.

On this dark cold February night, I found my way up Main Street, past the infamous Casino Club Bar where Hemingway and his cronies spent many a winter night and day drinking, carousing and having a high ol' time. Turning up Sun Valley Road, only one mile to the paradise I thought awaited me, I had no idea the level of disappointment I would soon experience.

We drove up to the famed Sun Valley Lodge that once played host to nearly every Hollywood star—from my favorite, Gary Cooper, to Clark Gable and Ingrid Bergman. Pick a name and it's certain they were guests here at one time or another. If it was good enough for Gary and his family, it was good enough for us I thought.

Checking in at the front desk was pleasant and uneventful, but I do remember asking a young French desk clerk how to get downtown. With a shy smile, he proudly announced, "You are downtown," and pointed in the direction of the lodge's front doors. Outside, past the geese squawking in the pond down the brick pathway, lay a quaint and somewhat charming shopping mall.

As we walked to our room, my heart sank, and I suggested to my wife that perhaps we made a mistake and grossly overestimated the allegedly great and historic Sun Valley. With considerable disappointment, we agreed to call our travel agent back in Chicago first thing in the morning to see if we could make arrangements to get us out of Sun Valley and get into Colorado on the first available flight.

It was still too early for sleep, so we wandered downstairs to the elegant Duchin Room, the hotel's legendary bar. I couldn't help but wonder why the wait staff was dressed in green Bavarian-style costumes. Only later I learned that this was a reflection of the original Austrian influence that shaped the Sun Valley Lodge resort experience.

Over strong drinks, we discussed our disappointment and forthcoming morning departure, hopefully to Colorado—a real vacation paradise. By the time we got back to our room, I found I still could not stop thinking about those green Bavarian outfits. Hadn't I seen them worn on one of those late-night war movies some time back? Oh well, I didn't need to think about that anymore since we were planning on being out of here in the morning.

The next day was Sunday. How lucky we were that we had no way to contact our travel agent back in Chicago. Awakening to a drop-dead-gorgeous sunny day, I soon discovered that first impressions can be dangerously deceiving. Looking out on Mt. Baldy, there was more than 3,000 acres of fabulously groomed runs and a charming town called Ketchum, with real shops, no geese, and welcoming locals.

Needless to say, our plans to leave faded and we drove into Ketchum where we experienced a town filled with people who welcomed us and were extremely friendly. "Maybe we didn't look like tourists," I thought. I must say, it felt really good and I quickly realized this was a special place after all.

Two weeks of great skiing, great meals and sightseeing passed before we could blink an eye, but not before we checked out all the art galleries in town and realized there was an obvious opportunity for me to open a gallery there. Before either of us could change our minds, we put a bid in on a house and I found retail space for my new gallery. Clearly we had fallen in love with the valley. Six months later, we were Idaho residents and our wilderness adventure began and continues to this day.

It has been an absolute joy and privilege to have met some of the most wonderful people, both clients and friends, since moving to Sun Valley. I have learned something from every one of you—not all of it good, but what the heck—you're forgiven.

I would like to thank all the homeowners and architects who have made this book possible. Your hospitality was invaluable in making this book a reality. I am truly grateful for your enthusiasm and participation in this project. I salute the extraordinary staff at Michel's Christiania Restaurant who provided us with the world's best Potato Vodka Martinis during pre-production meetings. We will see you all soon.

To my talented collaborators, Jo Rabjohn, Tim Brown and Mariel Hemingway, I thank you for your patience, determination and shared vision to produce a first-rate book. It has been a pleasure working with you. To our wonderful editor, Jennifer Maughan, I thank you for all your encouragement, guidance and many kind e-mails that kept us focused and on track. I owe a very special thank you to my friend and publisher, Gibbs Smith, a true Renaissance man, who from the very beginning gave me unwavering encouragement and support for this project.

Finally, I would like to say if you purchased this book, I thank you. You obviously have impeccable taste and great style. I hope you enjoy the homes pictured within, along with the collection of vintage photos, posters and historic memorabilia.

One last thought. If, after reading this book, any of you out there become really inspired and think of moving here, please don't. Trust me, there is nothing for miles except millions of potatoes. Colorado, on the other hand, is a real vacation paradise. Feel free to drop me a postcard from Aspen.

JO RABJOHN

I had only been living in the Wood River Valley a few months when I started writing this book. The adjustment was surprisingly easy in spite of the fact that my first visit to Sun Valley was bewildering. Ten minutes before my plane was to land we were turned back to Twin Falls, because of lack of visibility, to be bussed. There was a lot of moaning on the small commuter jet when the announcement was made. On the ride to Sun Valley I was expecting to wind through mountain passes and switch backs to a ski resort only to find us bussing along a straight road through desert and lava fields. Eventually the terrain became fertile farmland bordered by dramatic treeless mountains. Ahead the valley narrowed and rose in elevation. It was beautiful.

I am a sixth-generation Californian and when I returned from Sun Valley and told my father, Ray Rabjohn, of my decision to move to Idaho he replied, "You're moving back east?" The decision was impulsive and I purchased my home in the Wood River Valley sight unseen while still in California. I have not experienced buyer's remorse.

What has surprised me most is my contentment here. I have found a distillation of the best. Sun Valley has a plethora of art galleries, fine restaurants, concerts, theater and what appeared to be hand-picked retail and specialty shops. There are sporting goods merchants to supply every possible need to every sports person. I have found delight in the attitude and embracing of everyone's pet dog. People take their dogs everywhere, to work, parties, out to dinner, grocery stores, doctor's offices and every errand they might run. There is even a dog that goes to the movies. Then there is the matter of the three-legged dogs. They are frequently seen gimping along with their owners. Both of my neighbors on either side of my home have three-legged dogs. It's not exactly one of the mysteries of the East but it does give "paws" for thought.

The homes here in the valley that I have written about enchant me. Grand and modest homes sit in natural settings and use the prevailing landscape to dictate architecture and design. The drama of the geography influenced each and demanded a standard of excellence. Traditional log homes of grand proportions fit beautifully within this valley just as the bold and non-traditional homes find perfect placement. These homes truly reflect those who live in them. I would like to give thanks and appreciation to the owners of the properties showcased in this book. All were cordial and kind to open their houses to us, and we were overwhelmed by patience shown as the three of us invaded and prodded with questions.

To be relatively new to an area and be able to write about it has been a pleasure because of the people I have met. The Wood River Valley may be one of the most desirable locations geographically but it has been my pleasure to find the people its equal—gracious and hospitable.

I would like to express my appreciation to Alan Edison for giving me the opportunity to co-write this book. Jennifer Maughan, our editor, is to be thanked for her hard work. But nothing would have happened without Gibbs and Catherine Smith. They are a special blessing to me.